Manifesto for a European Renaissance

Manifesto
for a
European
Renaissance

Alain de Benoist
and
Charles Champetier

ARKTOS
London 2012

Published in 2012 by Arktos Media Ltd.

© 2012 Arktos Media Ltd.

No part of this book may be reproduced or utilised in any form or by
any means (whether electronic or mechanical), including photocopying,
recording or by any information storage and retrieval system, without
permission in writing from the publisher.

Printed in the United Kingdom

ISBN 978-1-907166-78-5

BIC classification: Social & political philosophy (HPS)
Conservatism and right-of-centre democratic ideologies (JPFM)
Nationalism (JPFN)

Editor: John B. Morgan
Cover Design & Layout: Daniel Friberg

ARKTOS MEDIA LTD

www.arktos.com

TABLE OF CONTENTS

EDITOR'S PREFACE

This manifesto was reprinted by the kind permission of Alain de Benoist. It was originally published in *Éléments* 94, February 1999, pp. 11-23, as 'Manifeste pour une renaissance européenne: À la découverte du GRECE, Son histoire, ses idées, son organisation'. This translation was published in *Telos* 115, Spring 1999, pp. 117-144, under the title 'The French New Right in the Year 2000', and is by Martin Bendelow and Francis Greene. *Telos* was also generous in allowing us to reprint their translation.

GRECE (Groupement de recherche et d'études pour la civilisation européenne, or Research Group for the Study of European Civilisation) was founded by Alain de Benoist and his colleagues in Paris in 1968 in an effort to revive and redefine certain political and cultural ideas which had been discredited since 1945 as a result of their supposed association with the fascist movements of that era. The term 'New Right' was a moniker which Benoist and his colleagues never applied to themselves, believing that their thought lay outside the traditional categories of what constitutes 'Left' and 'Right', although they have since come to grudgingly accept it. Benoist, and the then editor of Éléments, one of GRECE's periodicals, Charles Champetier, collaborated on this work in an effort to assess and summarize the first 30 years in the development of GRECE's thought, as well as to provide some guidance for its future direction at the dawn of the new millennium. It remains the only attempt by GRECE to date to outline the fundamental components of its philosophy. Since 1968 and continuing to the present day, GRECE's influence has spread throughout Europe and across the world.

Readers who wish to learn more about the ideas and history of the European New Right are urged to consult Tomislav Sunic's *Against Democracy and Equality: The European New Right* (London: Arktos, 2011) and Michael O'Meara's *New Culture, New Right: Anti-Liberalism in Postmodern Europe* (Bloomington: 1stBooks, 2004).

JOHN B. MORGAN IV
Bangalore, India,
May 2012

INTRODUCTION

The French New Right was born in 1968. It is not a political movement, but a think-tank and school of thought. For more than thirty years — in books and journals, colloquia and conferences, seminars and summer schools, etc. — it has attempted to formulate a metapolitical perspective.

Metapolitics is not politics by other means. It is neither a 'strategy' to impose intellectual hegemony, nor an attempt to discredit other possible attitudes or agendas. It rests solely on the premise that ideas play a fundamental role in collective consciousness and, more generally, in human history. Through their works, Heraclitus, Aristotle, St. Augustine, St. Thomas Aquinas, René Descartes, Immanuel Kant, Adam Smith, and Karl Marx all triggered decisive revolutions, whose impact is still being felt today. History is a result of human will and action, but always within the framework of convictions, beliefs and representations which provide meaning and direction. The goal of the French New Right is to contribute to the renewal of these sociohistorical representations.

Even more now, this metapolitical impulse is based on a reflection about the evolution of Western societies in view of the coming Twenty-first century. On the one hand, there is the growing impotence of political parties, unions, governments, classical forms of conquest and the exercise of political power, and, on the other, the rapid obsolescence of all antitheses (first and foremost, Left and Right) that have characterised modernity. Moreover, there is an unprecedented explosion of knowledge, which spreads with little regard for its consequences. In a world where closed entities have given way to interconnected networks with increasingly fuzzy reference points, metapolitical action attempts, beyond political divisions and through a new synthesis, to renew a transversal mode of thought and, ultimately, to study all areas of knowledge in order to propose a coherent worldview. Such has been the aim for over thirty years.

This manifesto summarises all of this. The first part ('Predicaments') provides a critical analysis of the present; the second part

('Foundations') outlines a view concerning man and the world. Both are inspired by a multidisciplinary approach that challenges most of today's intellectual antitheses. Tribalism and globalism, nationalism and internationalism, liberalism and Marxism, individualism and collectivism, progressivism and conservatism oppose each other with the same complacent logic of the excluded middle. For a century, these artificial oppositions have occluded what is most essential: the sheer size of a crisis that demands a radical renewal of modes of thought, decision and action. It is thus futile to seek this radical renewal in what has already been written. Yet, the French New Right has borrowed ideas from various theoretical sources. It has not hesitated to reappropriate what seems valuable in all currents of thought. This transverse approach has provoked the ire of the guardians of thought, concerned with freezing ideological orthodoxies in order to paralyse any new threatening synthesis.

From the very beginning, the French New Right has brought together people interested in participating in the development of a community. In France, as in other countries, it constitutes a community of work and reflection, whose members are not necessarily intellectuals, but all of whom are interested, in one way or another, in the battle of ideas. The third part of this manifesto ('Positions') takes positions on current issues, debates and the future of peoples and civilisation.

I. PREDICAMENTS

First and foremost, all critical thought attempts to put the age in which it develops in perspective. The present is a pivotal period — a turning point or an *interregnum*, characterised by a major crisis: the end of modernity.

1. What is Modernity?

Modernity designates the political and philosophical movement of the last three centuries of Western history. It is characterised primarily by five converging processes: *individualisation*, through the destruction of old forms of communal life; *massification*, through the adoption of standardised behaviour and lifestyles; *desacralisation*, through the displacement of the great religious narratives by a scientific interpretation of the world; *rationalisation*, through the domination of instrumental reason, the free market, and technical efficiency; and *universalisation*, through a planetary extension of a model of society postulated implicitly as the only rational possibility and thus as superior.

This movement has old roots. In most respects, it represents a secularisation of ideas and perspectives borrowed from Christian metaphysics, which spread into secular life following a rejection of any transcendent dimension. Actually, one finds in Christianity the seeds of the great mutations that gave birth to the secular ideologies of the first post-revolutionary era. Individualism was already present in the notion of individual salvation and of an intimate and privileged relation between an individual and God that surpasses any relation on Earth. Egalitarianism is rooted in the idea that redemption is equally available to all mankind, since all are endowed with an individual soul whose absolute value is shared by all humanity. Progressivism is born of the idea that history has an absolute beginning and a necessary end, and that it unfolds globally according to a divine plan. Finally, universalism is the natural expression of a religion that claims to manifest a revealed truth which, valid for all men, summons them to conversion. Modern political life itself is founded on secularised theological concepts. Reduced to an opinion among others, today Christianity has unwittingly become the victim of the movement it started. In the history of the West, it became the religion of the way out of religion.

The various concurrent and often contradictory philosophical schools of modernity agree on one issue: that there is a unique and universalisable solution for all social, moral and political problems. Humanity is understood to be the sum of rational individuals who, through self-interest, moral conviction, fellowship or even fear are called upon to realise their unity in history. In this perspective, the diversity of the world becomes an obstacle, and all that differentiates men is thought to be incidental or contingent, outmoded or even dangerous. To the extent that modernity is not only a body of ideas, but also a mode of action, it attempts by every available means to uproot individuals from their individual communities, to subject them to a universal mode of association. In practice, the most efficient means for doing this has been the marketplace.

2. The Crisis of Modernity

The imagery of modernity is dominated by desires of freedom and equality. These two cardinal values have been betrayed. Cut off from the communities which protected them, giving meaning and form to their existence, individuals are now subject to such an immense mechanism of domination and decision that their freedom remains purely formal. They endure the global power of the marketplace, techno-science, or communications without ever being able to influence their course. The promise of equality has failed on two counts: Communism has betrayed it by installing the most murderous totalitarian regimes in history; capitalism has trivialised it by legitimating the most odious social and economic inequalities in the name of equality. Modernity proclaims rights without in any way providing the means to exercise them. It exacerbates all needs and continually creates new ones, while reserving access to them to a small minority, which feeds the frustration and anger of all others. As for the ideology of progress, which responds to human expectations by nourishing the promise of an ever-improving world, it is in a deep crisis. The future appears unpredictable, no longer offering hope, and terrifying almost everyone. Each generation confronts a world different from the one its fathers knew. Combined with accelerated transformations of life-styles and living contexts (*nomoi*),[1] this enduring newness predicated on discrediting the fathers and old experiences, produces not happiness but misery.

The 'end of ideologies' is an expression designating the historical exhaustion of the great mobilising narratives that became embodied in liberalism, socialism, Communism, nationalism, Fascism, and, finally, Nazism. The Twentieth century has sounded the death knell for most of these doctrines, whose concrete results were genocide, ethnic cleansing, and mass murder, total wars among nations and permanent rivalry among individuals, ecological disasters, social chaos, and the loss of all significant reference points. The destruction of the life-world for the benefit of instrumental reason, (economic) growth, and material development have resulted in an unprecedented impoverishment of the spirit, and the generalisation of anxiety related to living in an always uncertain present, in a world deprived both of the past and the future. Thus, modernity has given birth to the most empty civilisation mankind has ever known: the language of advertising has become the paradigm of all social discourse; the primacy of money has imposed the omnipresence of commodities; man has been transformed into an object of exchange in a context of mean hedonism; technology has ensnared the life-world in a network of rationalism — a world replete with delinquency, violence, and incivility, in which man is at war with himself and against all, i.e., an unreal world of drugs, virtual reality and media-hyped sports, in which the countryside is abandoned for unliveable suburbs and monstrous megalopolises, and where the solitary individual merges into an anonymous and hostile crowd, while traditional social, political, cultural or religious mediations become increasingly uncertain and undifferentiated.

This general crisis is a sign that modernity is reaching its end, precisely when the universalist utopia that established it is poised to become a reality under the form of liberal globalisation. The end of the Twentieth century marks both the end of modern times and the beginning of a postmodernity characterised by a series of new themes: preoccupation with ecology, concern for the quality of life, the role of 'tribes' and of 'networks', revival of communities, the politics of group identities, multiplication of intra- and supra-state conflicts, the return of social violence, the decline of established religions, growing

---

1   *Nomoi*, from the ancient Greek, refers to a system of rules enforced by an institution. -Ed.

opposition to social elitism, etc. Having nothing new to say, and observing the growing malaise of contemporary societies, the agents of the dominant ideology are reduced to the cliché-ridden discourse so common in the media in a world threatened by implosion — *implosion*, not explosion, because modernity will not be transcended with a *grand soir*[2] (a secular version of the Second Coming of Christ), but with the appearance of thousands of auroras, i.e., the birth of sovereign spaces liberated from the domination of the modern. Modernity will not be transcended by returning to the past, but by means of certain premodern values in a decisively postmodern dimension. It is only at the price of such a radical restructuring that anomie and contemporary nihilism will be exorcised.

3. Liberalism: The Main Enemy

Liberalism embodies the dominant ideology of modernity. It was the first to appear and will be the last to disappear. In the beginning, liberal thought contraposed an autonomous economy to the morality, politics and society in which it had been formerly embedded. Later, it turned commercial value into the essence of all communal life. The advent of the 'primacy of quantity' signalled this transition from market economics to market societies, i.e., the extension of the laws of commercial exchange, ruled by the 'invisible hand', to all spheres of existence. On the other hand, liberalism also engendered modern individualism, both from a false anthropology and from the descriptive as well as normative view based on a one-dimensional man drawing his 'inalienable rights' from his essentially asocial nature continually trying to maximise his best interest by eliminating any non-quantifiable consideration and any value unrelated to rational calculation.

This dual individualistic and economic impulse is accompanied by a Darwinian social vision which, in the final analysis, reduces social life to a generalised competition, to a new version of a 'war of all against all' to select the 'best'. Aside from the fact that 'pure and perfect' competition is a myth, since there are always power relations, it says absolutely nothing about the value of what is chosen: what is better or worse. Evolution selects those most apt to survive. But man is not

---

2   French: 'big night', as in when a significant event happens, such as a large celebration. -Ed.

satisfied with mere survival: he orders his life in a hierarchy of values about which liberals claim to remain neutral.

In the Twentieth century, the iniquitous character of liberal domination generated a legitimate reaction: the appearance of the socialist movement. Under the influence of Marxism, however, this movement became misdirected. Yet, despite their mutual hostility, liberalism and Marxism basically belong to the same universe and are both the heirs of Enlightenment thought: they share the same individualism, even the same universal egalitarianism, the same rationalism, the same primacy of economics, the same stress on the emancipatory value of labour, the same faith in progress, the same idea of an end of history. In almost all respects, liberalism has only realised more effectively certain objectives it shares with Marxism: the eradication of collective identities and traditional cultures, the disenchantment of the world, and the universalisation of the system of production.

The ravages of the market have also triggered the rise and growth of the welfare state. Throughout history, the market and the state have appeared on an equal footing, the latter seeking to subject inter-communal, non-market exchange, which is intangible, to the law of money, and to turn homogeneous economic space into a tool of its power. The dissolution of communal bonds, spurred by the commercialisation of social life, has necessitated the progressive strengthening of the welfare state, since it is entrusted with the redistribution necessary to mitigate the failures of traditional solidarity. Far from hindering liberalism, these statist interventions have allowed it to prosper by avoiding a social explosion, thus generating the security and stability indispensable to exchange. In return, the welfare state, which is nothing but an abstract, anonymous and opaque redistributive structure, has generalised irresponsibility, transforming the members of society into nothing more than recipients of public assistance, who no longer seek to overthrow the liberal system, but only to prolong the indefinite extension of rights with no *quid pro quo*.

Finally, liberalism denies the specificity of politics, which always implies arbitrariness of decisions and plurality of goals. From this viewpoint, the term 'liberal politics' appears to be a contradiction in terms. Seeking to form social bonds on the basis of a theory of rational choice that reduces citizenship to utility, it ends up with an ideal 'scientific' management of global society by technical experts. The liberal state, all too often synonymous with a republic of judges, is committed to the parallel goals of abstaining from proposing a model of the good life while seeking to neutralise conflicts inherent in the diversity of social life by pursuing policies aimed at determining, by purely juridical procedures, what is just rather than what is good. The public sphere dissolves into the private, while representative democracy is reduced to a market in which supply becomes increasingly limited (concentration of programs and convergence of policies) and demand less and less motivated (abstention).

In the age of globalisation, liberalism no longer presents itself as an ideology, but as a global system of production and reproduction of men and commodities, supplemented by the hypermodernism of human rights. In its economic, political and moral forms, liberalism represents the central bloc of the ideas of a modernity that is finished. Thus, it is the main obstacle to anything seeking to go beyond it.

II. FOUNDATIONS

'Know thyself', said the oracle of Delphi. The key to any representation of the world, to any political, moral or philosophical engagement is, first of all, an anthropology, whereby activities are carried out through certain practical orders, which represent the essence of peoples' relations among themselves and with the world: politics, economics, technology, and ethics.

1. Man: An Aspect of Life

Modernity has denied any human nature (the theory of the *tabula rasa*) or it has related it back to abstract attributes disconnected from the real world and lived experience. As a consequence of this radical rupture, the ideal of a 'new man', infinitely malleable through the brutal and progressive transformation of his environment, has emerged. In the Twentieth century, this utopia has resulted in totalitarianism and the concentration camps. In the liberal world, it has translated into the superstitious belief in an all-powerful environment, which has generated deceptions, in particular in the educational sphere: in a society structured by abstract rationality, cognitive ability is the main determinant of social status.

Man is first and foremost an animal. He exists as such in the order of living beings, which is measured in hundreds of millions of years. If one compares the history of organic life to one day (twenty-four hours), the human species appeared only in the last thirty seconds. The process of humanisation has unfolded over umpteen thousands of generations. To the extent that life is generated above all through the transmission of information contained in genetic material, man is not born like a blank page: every single individual already bears the general characteristics of the species, to which are added specific hereditary predispositions to certain particular aptitudes and modes of behaviour. The individual does not decide this inheritance, which limits his autonomy and his plasticity, but also allows him to resist political and social conditioning.

But man is not just an animal: what is specifically human in him — consciousness of his own consciousness, abstract thought, syntactic language, the capacity for symbolism, the aptitude for objective observation and value judgment — does not contradict his nature, but extends it by conferring on him a supplementary and unique identity. To deny man's biological determinants or to reduce them by relegating his specific traits to zoology is absurd. The hereditary part of humanity forms only the basis of social and historical life: human instincts are not programmed in their object, i.e., man always has the freedom to make choices, moral as well as political, which naturally are limited only by death. Man is an heir, but he can dispose of his heritage. He can construct himself historically and culturally on the basis of the presuppositions of his biological constitution, which are his human limitations. What lies beyond these limitations may be called God, the cosmos, nothingness, or Being. The question of 'why' no longer makes sense, because what is beyond human limitations is by definition unthinkable.

Thus, the New Right proposes a vision of a well-balanced individual, taking into account both inborn, personal abilities and the social environment. It rejects ideologies that emphasise only one of these factors, be it biological, economic, or mechanical.

2. Man: A Rooted, Imperilled, and Open Being

By nature, man is neither good nor bad, but he is capable of being either one or the other. As an open and imperilled being, he is always able to go beyond himself or to debase himself. Man can keep this permanent threat at bay by constructing social and moral rules, as well as institutions and traditions, which provide a foundation for his existence and give his life meaning and references. Defined as the undifferentiated mass of individuals that constitutes it, humanity designates either a biological category (the species) or a philosophical category emanating from Western thought. From the socio-historical viewpoint, man as such does not exist, because his membership within humanity is always mediated by a particular cultural belonging. This observation does not stem from relativism. All men have in common their human nature, without which they would not be able to understand each other, but their common membership in the species always expresses itself in a single *context*. They share the same essential aspirations, which are always crystallised in different forms according to time and place.

In this sense, humanity is irreducibly plural: diversity is part of its very essence. Thus, human life is necessarily rooted in a given context, prior to the way individuals and groups see the world, even critically, and to the way they formulate their aspirations and goals. They do not exist in the real world other than as concretely rooted people. Biological differences are significant only in reference to social and cultural givens. As for differences between cultures, they are the effects neither of illusion nor of transitory, contingent or secondary characteristics. All cultures have their own 'centre of gravity' (Herder): different cultures provide different responses to essential questions. This is why all attempts to unify them end up destroying them. Man is rooted by nature in his culture. He is a singular being: he always locates himself at the interface of the universal (his species) and the particular (each culture, each epoch). Thus, the idea of an absolute, universal, and eternal law that ultimately determines moral, religious, or political choices appears unfounded. This idea is the basis of all totalitarianisms.

Human societies are both conflictual and cooperative, without being able to eliminate one to the benefit of the other. The ironic belief in the possibility of eliminating these antagonisms within a transparent and reconciled society has no more validity than the hyper-competitive (liberal, racist, or nationalist) vision that turns life into a perpetual war of individuals or groups. If aggressiveness is an essential part of the creativity and dynamism of life, evolution has also favoured in man the emergence of cooperative (altruistic) behaviours evident not only in the sphere of genetic kinship. On the other hand, great historical constructions have been possible only by establishing a harmony based on the recognition of the common good, the reciprocity of rights and duties, cooperation and sharing. Neither peaceful nor belligerent, neither good nor bad, neither beautiful nor ugly, human existence unfolds in a tragic tension between these poles of attraction and repulsion.

3. Society: A Body of Communities

Human existence is inseparable from the communities and social groups in which it reveals itself. The idea of a primitive 'state of nature' in which autonomous individuals might have coexisted is pure fiction:

society is not the result of a contract between men trying to maximise their best interests, but rather of a spontaneous association whose most ancient form is undoubtedly the extended family.

The communities within which society is grounded are constituted by a complex net of intermediary bodies situated among individuals, groups of individuals, and humanity. Some are inherited (native), others are chosen (cooperative). The social bond, whose autonomy the classical Right parties have never recognised, and which should not be confused with 'civil society', is defined, first and foremost, as a model for individual actions, not as the global effect of these actions. It rests on shared consent and is prior to this model. Membership in the collective does not destroy individual identity; rather, it is the basis for it. When one leaves one's original community, it is generally to join another one. Native or cooperative communities are all based on reciprocity. Communities are constituted and maintain themselves on the basis of who belongs to them. Membership is all that is required. There is a vertical reciprocity of rights and duties, contributions and distributions, obedience and assistance, and a horizontal reciprocity of gifts, fraternity, friendship, and love. The richness of social life is proportional to the diversity of the members: this diversity is constantly threatened either by shortcomings (conformity, lack of differentiation) or excesses (secession, atomisation).

The holistic conception, where the whole exceeds the sum of its parts and possesses qualities none of its individual parts have, has been defeated by modern universalism and individualism, which have associated community with the ideas of submission to hierarchy, entanglement, or parochialism. This universalism and individualism have been deployed in two ways: the contract (politics) and the market (economics). But, in reality, modernity has not liberated man from his original familial belonging or from local, tribal, corporative or religious attachments. It has only submitted him to other constraints, which are harsher, because they are further away, more impersonal, and more demanding: a mechanistic, abstract, and homogeneous subjugation has replaced multiform organic modes. In becoming more solitary, man also has become more vulnerable and more destitute. He has become disconnected from meaning, because he can no longer identify himself with a model, and because there is no longer any way for him to understand his place in the social whole. Individualism has resulted in disaffiliation, separation, deinstitutionalisation (thus, the family no longer socialises), and the appropriation of the social bond by statist bureaucracies. In the final analysis, the great project of modern emancipation has resulted only in generalised alienation. Because modern societies tend to bring together individuals who experience each other as strangers, no longer having any mutual confidence, they cannot envision a social relation not subject to a 'neutral' regulatory authority. The pure forms are exchange (a market system of the rule of the strongest) and submission (the totalitarian system of obedience to the all-powerful state). The mixed form that now prevails is a proliferation of abstract juridical rules that gradually intersect every area of existence, whereby relations with others are permanently controlled in order to ward off the threat of implosion. Only a return to communities and to a politics of human dimensions can remedy exclusion or dissolution of the social bond, its reification, and its juridification.

4. Politics: An Essence and an Art

Politics is consistent with the fact that the goals of social life are always multiple. Its essence and its laws cannot be reduced to economics, ethics, aesthetics, metaphysics, or the sacred. It both acknowledges and distinguishes between such notions as public and private, command and obedience, deliberation and decision, citizen and foreigner, friend and enemy. If there is morality in politics, since authority aims at a common good and is inspired by the collectivity's values and customs, this does not mean that an individual morality is politically applicable. Regimes which refuse to recognise the essence of politics, which deny the plurality of goals or favour depoliticisation, are by definition 'unpolitical'.

Modern thought has developed the illusion of politics as 'neutral', reducing power to managerial efficiency, to the mechanical application of juridical, technical or economic norms: the 'government of men' ought to be modelled on the 'administration of things'. The public sphere, however, always affirms a particular vision of the 'good life'. This idea of the 'good' precedes the idea of the 'just' — not the other way around.

Domestically, the first aim of all political action is civil peace: internally, security and harmony between all members of society; externally, protection from foreign danger. Compared with this aim, the choice between values such as liberty, equality, unity, diversity and solidarity is arbitrary: it is not self-evident, but is a matter of the end result. Diversity of worldviews is one of the conditions for the emergence of politics. Because it recognises the pluralism of aspirations and projects, democracy seeks to facilitate peaceful confrontations at all levels of public life; it is an eminently political form of government. If the individual considers himself to be part of a community, then he will behave as a citizen in a democracy, which is the only form of government that offers him participation in public discussions and decisions, as well as the ability to make something of himself and to excel through education. Politics is not a science, given over to reason or technology, but an art, calling for prudence before everything else. It always implies uncertainty, a plurality of choices, a decision about goals. The art of governing provides the power to arbitrate between various possibilities, along with the capacity for constraint. Power is never merely a *means* that has value only as a function of the goals it is supposed to serve.

According to Jean Bodin, heir of the French jurists of the Middle Ages (the *légistes*), the source of independence and liberty resides in the prince's unlimited sovereignty, modelled after papal absolutist power. This is the concept of a 'political theology' based on the idea of a supreme political organ — a 'Leviathan' (Hobbes) — charged with controlling body, spirit and soul. It inspired the unified and centralised absolutist nation-state, which tolerated neither local power nor the sharing of law with neighbouring territorial powers. It was developed through administrative and judicial unification, the elimination of intermediary bodies (denounced as 'feudal'), and the gradual eradication of all local cultures. Eventually, it became absolutist monarchy, revolutionary Jacobinism, and, finally, modern totalitarianism. But it also led to a 'republic without citizens', in which there is nothing left between atomised civil society and the managerial state. To this model of political society, the French New Right contraposes the legacy of Althusius,[3] where the source of independence and liberty resides in

---

3   Johannes Althusius (1563-1638) was a political philosopher who is credited with having formulated the idea of federalism, by which autonomous groups which retain local authority are bound together with others to form a common whole, with only some powers delegated to the central authority. His ideas were also crucial to the idea of subsidiarity in politics. An essay by de Benoist on Althusius, entitled 'The First Federalist', was published in *Telos* 118, Winter 2000. -Ed.

autonomy, and the state defines itself first and foremost as a federation of organised communities and multiple allegiances.

In this view, which has inspired both imperial and federal constructions, the existence of a delegation of sovereign powers never results in the people losing their ability to make or abrogate laws. In their variously organised collectivities, the people (or 'states') are the ultimate repository of sovereignty. The rulers are above each citizen individually, but they are always subordinate to the general will expressed by the body of citizens. The principle of subsidiarity rules at all levels. The liberty of a collectivity is not antithetical to shared sovereignty. Ultimately, politics is not reduced to the level of the state: the public person is defined as a complex of groups, families and associations, of local, regional, national or supranational collectivities. Politics does not deny this organic continuity, but takes its support from it. Political unity proceeds from a recognised diversity, i.e., it must admit that there is something 'opaque' in the social fabric: the perfect 'transparency' of society is a utopia that does not encourage democratic communication; on the contrary, it favours totalitarian surveillance.

5. Economics: Beyond the Marketplace

As far as one goes back into the history of human societies, certain rules have presided over the production, circulation and consummation of the goods necessary to the survival of individuals and groups. For all that, and contrary to the presuppositions of liberalism and Marxism, the economy has never formed the infrastructure of society: economic over-determination ('economism') is the exception, not the rule. Moreover, numerous myths associated with the curses of labour (Prometheus, rape of the Mother-Earth), money (Croesus, Gullveig, Tarpeia), and abundance (Pandora) reveal that early on the economy was perceived as the 'damned part' of all society, as an activity that threatened to destroy all harmony. The economy was thus devalued, not because it was not useful, but for the simple reason that it was only that. What is more, one was rich because one was powerful, and not the reverse, power being thus matched by a duty to share and to protect those under one's care. The 'fetishism of commodities' as a peculiarity of modern capitalism was clearly recognised as a danger: production of abundance of different goods arouses envy, the mimetic desire, which in turn generates disorder and violence.

In all pre-modern societies, the economic was embedded and con-textualised within other orders of human activity (Karl Polanyi).[4] The idea that economic exchange from barter to the modern market always has been regulated by the confrontation of supply and demand, by the consequent emergence of an equivalent abstract (money) and of objective values (use values, exchange values, utility, etc.) is a fairy-tale invented by liberalism. The market is not an ideal model whose abstraction allows universalisation. Before being a mechanism, it is an institution, and this institution can be abstracted neither from its his-tory nor from the cultures that have generated it.

The three great forms of the circulation of goods are reciprocity (mutual gift-giving, equal or joint sharing), redistribution (centralisa-tion and distribution by a single authority), and exchange. They do not represent stages of development, but have more or less always coex-isted. Modern society is characterised by a hypertrophy of free mar-ket exchange, leading from an economy *with* a market, to a market society. The liberal economy has translated the ideology of progress into a religion of growth: the 'ever more' of consumption is supposed to lead humanity to happiness. While it is undeniable that modern economic development has satisfied certain primary needs of a much larger number of people than previously possible, it is not any less true that the artificial growth of needs through the seductive strategies of the system of objects (advertising) necessarily ends in an impasse. In a world of finite resources, subject to the principle of entropy, a certain slowing of growth prefigures humanity's inevitable horizon.

Given the breadth of transformations it has brought about, the commodification of the world from the Sixteenth to the Twentieth century has been one of the most important phenomena in human history. Decommodification will be one of the main phenomena in the Twenty-first century. Thus, it is necessary to return to the origins of the economy (*oikos-nomos*),[5] to the general laws of the human habitat in the world, which include those of ecological balance, human pas-sion, respect for the harmony and beauty of nature, and, in a more general way, all the non-quantifiable elements that economic science

4   Karl Polanyi (1886-1964) was an Austrian sociologist who saw the rise of the mod-ern nation-state as the inevitable result of the development of the market econo-my, as argued in his book *The Great Transformation*. -Ed.

5   Greek: 'household economics', the term from which the word 'economics' is de-rived. -Ed.

has arbitrarily excluded from its calculations. All economic life implies the mediation of a large range of cultural institutions and juridical means. Today, the economy must be recontextualised within life, society, politics and ethics.

6. Ethics: The Construction of Oneself

The fundamental categories of ethics are universal: the distinctions between noble and ignoble, good and bad, admirable and despicable, just and unjust can be found everywhere. On the other hand, the designation and evaluation of behaviours relevant to each of these categories varies with epochs and societies. The French New Right rejects all purely moral views of the world, but it recognises that no culture can avoid distinguishing between the ethical values of various attitudes and behaviours. Morality is indispensable to this open being that is man; it is an anthropological consequence of his freedom. In articulating general rules necessary for the survival of any society, moral codes become attached to customs (*mores*), and cannot be dissociated completely from the context in which they are practiced. But they cannot be seen only in terms of subjectivity. Thus, the adage 'my country, right or wrong' does not mean that my country is always right, but that it remains my country even when it is wrong. This implies that I might eventually prove it wrong, which would mean that I subscribe to a norm beyond my belonging to it.

Since the Greeks, ethics for Europeans have designated virtues whose practice forms the basis of the 'good life': generosity over avarice, honour over shame, courage over cowardice, justice over injustice, temperance over excess, duty over irresponsibility, rectitude over guile, unselfishness over greed, etc. The good citizen is one who always tries to strive for excellence in each of these virtues (Aristotle). This will to excellence does not in any way exclude the existence of several modes of life (contemplative, active, productive, etc.), each arising from different moral codes, and each finding their place in the city's hierarchy. For example, European tradition, expressed in the ancient tripartite model, made wisdom prevail over force, and force over wealth. Modernity has supplanted traditional ethics, at once aristocratic and popular, by two kinds of bourgeois moral codes: the utilitarian (Bentham), based on the materialist calculation of pleasure and pain (what is good is what increases pleasure for the greatest number);

and the deontological morality (Kant), based on a unitary conception of the just, toward which all individuals must strive in accord with a universal moral law. This last approach supports the ideology of human rights, which is at once a minimal moral code and a strategic weapon of Western ethnocentrism. This ideology is a contradiction in terms. All men have rights, but they would not know how to be entitled to them as isolated beings; a right expresses a relation of equity, which implies the social. Thus, no right is conceivable outside a specific context in which to define it, outside a society to recognise it and to define the duties which represent the counterpart to it, and the means of constraint sufficient to apply it. As for fundamental liberties, they are not decreed, but they must be conquered and guaranteed. The fact that Europeans have imposed by force a right to autonomy does not in any way imply that all the peoples of the planet must be held responsible for guaranteeing rights in the same way.

Against the 'moral order', which confuses the social with the moral norm, ultimately Europeans must sustain the plurality of forms of social life, and think together about order and its opposite, Apollo and Dionysius. One can only avoid the relativism and nihilism of the 'last man' (Nietzsche), who today reveals himself against the background of practical materialism, by restoring some meaning, i.e., by retrieving some shared values, and by assuming some concrete certainties that have been tried and defended by self-conscious communities.

7. Technology: The Mobilisation of the World

Technology has been around from the very beginning; the absence of specific natural defences, the deprogramming of instincts, and the development of cognitive capacities have proceeded apace with the transformation of the environment. But technology has long been regulated by non-technological imperatives: by the necessary harmony of man, city and cosmos, as well as by respect for nature as the home of Being, submission of Promethean power, Olympian wisdom, repudiation of *hubris*, concern for quality rather than productivity, etc.

The technological explosion of modernity is explained by the disappearance of ethical, symbolic or religious codes. It finds its distant roots in the Biblical imperative: 'replenish the earth, and subdue it' (*Genesis*), which two millennia later Descartes revived when he urged man to 'make himself the master and owner of nature'. The dual theocentric split between the uncreated being and the created world is thus metamorphosed into a dual anthropocentric split between subject and object, the second unreservedly subjugated by the first. Modernity also has subjected science (the contemplative) to the technological (the operative), giving birth to an integrated 'techno-science', whose only reason for being is accelerating ever more the transformation of the world. In the Twentieth century, there have been more upheavals than during the previous 15,000 years. For the first time in human history, each new generation is obliged to integrate itself into a world that the preceding one has not experienced.

Technology develops essentially as an autonomous system: every new discovery is immediately absorbed into the global power of the operative, which makes it more complex and reinforces it. Recent developments in information technology (cybernetics and computers) are accelerating this systemic integration at a prodigious rate, the Internet being the most well-known. This network has neither a centre of decision-making nor one of entry and exit, but it maintains and constantly expands the interaction of millions of terminals connected to it.

Technology is not neutral; it obeys a number of values that guide its course: operability, efficiency, and performance. Its axiom is simple: everything that is possible can and will be realised effectively, the general belief being that additional technology will be able to rectify the defects of existing technology. Politics, the moral code, and law intervene *only afterwards* to judge the desirable or undesirable effects of innovation. The cumulative nature of techno-scientific development, which experiences periods of stagnation but not regression, has long supported the ideology of progress by demonstrating the growth of the powers of man over nature, and by reducing risks and uncertainties. Thus, technology has given humanity new means of existence, but at the same time it has led to a loss of the reason for living, since the future seems to depend only on the indefinite extension of the rational mastering of the world. The resulting impoverishment is more and increasingly perceived as the disappearance of an authentically human life on earth. Having explored the infinitely small and then the infinitely large, techno-science now is tackling man himself, at once the subject and the object of his own manipulations (cloning, artificial procreation, genetic fingerprinting, etc.). Man is becoming the simple extension of the tools he has created, adopting a technomorphic mentality that increases his vulnerability.

Technophobia and technophilia are equally unacceptable. Knowledge and its application are not to blame, but innovation is not desirable simply because of its novelty. Against scientific reductionism, arrogant positivism and obtuse obscurantism, technological development should follow from social, ethical and political choices, as well as anticipations (the principle of prudence), and should be reintegrated within the context of a vision of the world as *pluriversum*[6] and continuum.

8. The World: A Pluriversum

Diversity is inherent in the very movement of life, which flourishes as it becomes more complex. The plurality and variety of races, ethnic groups, languages, customs, even religions has characterised the development of humanity since the very beginning. Consequently, two attitudes are possible. For one, this biocultural diversity is a burden, and one must always and everywhere reduce men to what they have in common, a process which cannot avoid generating a series of perverse effects. For the other, this diversity is to be welcomed, and should be maintained and cultivated. The French New Right is profoundly opposed to the suppression of differences. It believes that a good system is one that transmits at least as much diversity as it has received. The true wealth of the world is first and foremost the diversity of its cultures and peoples.

The West's conversion to universalism has been the main cause of its subsequent attempt to *convert* the rest of the world: in the past, to its religion (the Crusades); yesterday, to its political principles (colonialism); and today, to its economic and social model (development) or its moral principles (human rights). Undertaken under the aegis of missionaries, armies, and merchants, the Westernisation of the planet has represented an imperialist movement fed by the desire to erase all otherness by imposing on the world a supposedly superior model invariably presented as 'progress'. Homogenising universalism is only

---

6   As opposed to a *universum*, which denotes something that is present everywhere, a *pluriversum* was defined by Julien Freund as a 'plurality of particular and independent collectivities or of divergent interpretations of the same universal idea' ('Schmitt's Political Thought', *Telos* 102, Winter 1995, p. 11). -Ed.

the projection and the mask of an ethnocentrism extended over the whole planet.

Westernisation and globalisation have modified the way the world is perceived. Primitive tribes called themselves 'men', implying that they considered themselves their species' only representatives. A Greek and a Chinese, a Russian and an Inca could live in the same epoch without being conscious of each other's existence. Those times are past. Given the West's pretense to make the world over in its own image, the current age is a new one in which ethnic, historical, linguistic or cultural differences coexist fully aware of their identity and the otherness that reflects it. For the first time in history, the world is a *pluriversum*, a multipolar order in which great cultural groups find themselves confronting one another in a shared global temporality, i.e., in a zero hour. Yet, modernisation is gradually becoming disconnected from Westernisation: new civilisations are gradually acquiring modern means of power and knowledge without renouncing their historical and cultural heritage for the benefit of Western ideologies and values.

The idea of an 'end of history', characterised by the global triumph of market rationality by generalising the lifestyle and political forms of the liberal West, is obviously false. On the contrary, a new '*Nomos* of the Earth'[7] is emerging — a new organisation of international relations. Antiquity and the Middle Ages saw an unequal development of the great autarchic civilisations. The Renaissance and the Classical Age were marked by the emergence and consolidation of nation-states in competition for the mastery, first of Europe, then of the world. The Twentieth century witnessed the development of a bipolar world in which liberalism and Marxism confronted each other, the maritime American power and the continental Soviet power. The Twenty-first century will be characterised by the development of a multipolar world of emerging civilisations: European, North American, South American, Arabic-Muslim, Chinese, Indian, Japanese, etc. These civilisations will not supplant the ancient local, tribal, provincial or national roots, but will be constituted as the ultimate collective form with which individuals are able to identify in addition to their common humanity. They will probably be called upon to collaborate in certain areas to

---

7 'The *nomos* of the Earth' was a term coined by Carl Schmitt to describe the expansion of European ideas of government throughout the world, and the subsequent construction of an international system based on them. He also authored a book by this title. -Ed.

defend humanity's common interests, notably with respect to ecology. In a multipolar world, power is defined as the ability to resist the influence of others rather than to impose one's own. The main enemy of this pluriverse will be any civilisation pretending to be universal and regarding itself entrusted with a redeeming mission ('Manifest Destiny') to impose its model on all others.

9. The Cosmos: A Continuum

The French New Right adheres to a unitary worldview, the matter and form of which only constitute variations on the same theme. The world is at once a unity and a multiplicity, integrating different levels of the visible and the invisible, different perceptions of time and space, different laws of organisation of its constituent elements. Microcosm and macrocosm interpenetrate and interact with one another. Thus, the French New Right rejects the absolute distinction between created and uncreated being, as well as the idea that this world is only the reflection of another world. The cosmos (*phusis*) is the place where Being manifests itself, the place where the truth (*aletheia*) of mutual belonging in this cosmos reveals itself. *Panta rhei* (Heraclitus): the opening to all is in everything.

Man finds and gives sense to his life only by adhering to what is greater than himself, what transcends the limits of his constitution. The French New Right fully recognises this anthropological constant, which manifests itself in all religions. It believes the return of the sacred will be accomplished by returning to some founding myths, and by the disappearance of false dichotomies: subject and object, body and thought, soul and spirit, essence and existence, rationality and sensibility, myth and logic, nature and supernatural, etc.

The disenchantment of the world translates into the closure of the modern spirit, which is incapable of projecting itself above and beyond its materialism and constituent anthropocentrism. Today's epoch has transferred the ancient divine attributes to the human subject (the metaphysics of subjectivity), thereby transforming the world into an object, i.e., into an agglomeration of means at the unlimited disposal of its ends. This ideal of reducing the world to utilitarian reason has been coupled with a linear concept of history endowed with a beginning (state of nature, paradise on earth, golden age, primitive communism, etc.) and an equally necessary end (a classless society, the reign of God, the ultimate stage of progress, entry into an era of pure rationality, transparent and conciliatory).

For the French New Right past, present, and future are not distinct moments of a directional and vectored history, but permanent dimensions of all lived moments. The past as well as the future always remain present in all their actuality. This presence — a fundamental category of time — is opposed to absence: forgetfulness of origins and occlusion of the horizon. This view of the world already found expression in European Antiquity, both in cosmological histories and in pre-Socratic thought. The 'paganism' of the French New Right articulates nothing more than sympathy for this ancient conception of the world, always alive in hearts and minds precisely because it does not belong to yesterday, but is eternal. Confronted with the *ersatz* sectarianism of fallen religions, as well as with certain neo-pagan parodies from the times of confusion, the French New Right is imbued with a very long memory: it maintains a relation to the beginning that harbours a sense of what is coming.

III. POSITIONS

1. Against Indifferentiation and Uprooting; For Clear and Strong Identities

The unprecedented menace of homogenisation which looms over the entire world leads to the pathological identities: bloody irredentisms, convulsive and chauvinistic nationalism, savage tribalisations, etc. Responsibility for these deplorable attitudes stems primarily from globalisation (political, economic, technological, and financial), which produced these attitudes in the first place. By denying individuals the right to locate themselves within a collective and historical identity, by imposing a uniform mode of representation, the Western system has given birth to unhealthy forms of self-affirmation. Fear of the 'Same' has replaced fear of the 'Other'. In France, this situation is aggravated by a crisis of the State which, for two centuries, has been the main symbolic social producer. Thus, the current weakening of the state has produced a greater void in France than in other Western nations.

The question of identity will assume even greater importance in the decades ahead. In undermining social systems that used to ascribe individuals their place in a clearly understood social order, modernity has actually encouraged questioning identity and has stirred up a desire for reliance and recognition in the public scene. But modernity has not been able to satisfy this need for identity. 'Worldwide tourism' is merely a pathetic alternative to withdrawing into one's own shell.

In regard to universalist utopias and the withering of traditional identities, the French New Right affirms the primacy of differences, which are neither transitory features leading to some higher form of unity, nor incidental aspects of private life. Rather, these differences are the very substance of social life. They can be native (ethnic, linguistic), but also political. Citizenship implies belonging, allegiance and participation in public life at different levels. Thus, one can be, at one and the same time, a citizen of one's neighbourhood, city, region, nation, and of Europe, according to the nature of power devolved to each of these levels of sovereignty. By contrast, one cannot be a citizen of the world, for the 'world' is not a political category. Wanting to be a citizen of the world is to link citizenship to an abstraction drawn from the vocabulary of the Liberal New Class.

The French New Right upholds the cause of peoples, because the right to difference is a principle which has significance only in terms of its generality. One is only justified in defending one's difference from others if one is also able to defend the difference of others. This means, then, that the right to difference cannot be used to exclude others who are different. The French New Right upholds equally ethnic groups, languages, and regional cultures under the threat of extinction, as well as native religions. The French New Right supports peoples struggling against Western imperialism.

2. Against Racism; For the Right to Difference

The term racism cannot be defined as a preference for endogamy, which arises from freedom of choice of individuals and of peoples. The Jewish people, for instance, owe their survival to their rejection of mixed marriages. Confronted with positions that are often simplistic, propagandist, or moralising, it is necessary to come back to the real meaning of words: racism is a theory which postulates that there are qualitative inequalities between the races, such that, on the whole, one can distinguish races as either 'superior' or 'inferior'; that an individual's value is deduced entirely from the race to which he belongs; or, that race constitutes the central determining factor in human history. These three postulates may be held together or separately. All three are false. If existing races vary from one another as regards this or that statistically isolated criterion, there is no absolute qualitative difference among them. Nor is there a global paradigm outside mankind that would permit creating a racial hierarchy. Finally, it is evident that an individual receives his worth from those qualities which are his own. Racism is not a disease of the mind, generated by prejudice or 'pre-modern' superstition. (Such an explanation is a liberal fable suggesting irrationality as the source of all social ills.) Rather, racism is an erroneous doctrine, one rooted in time, which finds its source in scientific positivism, according to which one can 'scientifically' measure with absolute certainty the value of human societies, and in social evolutionism, which tends to describe the history of humanity as a single, unified history, divided into 'stages' corresponding to various states of progress. (Thus certain peoples are seen as temporarily or permanently more 'advanced' than others.)

In contrast to racism, there is a universalist and a differentialist anti-racism. The former leads to the same conclusions as does the racism it denounces. As opposed to differences as is racism, universalist anti-racism only acknowledges in peoples their common belonging to a particular species and it tends to consider their specific identities as transitory or of secondary importance. By reducing the 'Other' to the 'Same' through a strictly assimilationist perspective, universalist anti-racism is, by definition, incapable of recognising or respecting otherness for what it is. Differentialist anti-racism, to which the New Right subscribes holds that the irreducible plurality of the human species constitutes a veritable treasure. Differentialist anti-racism makes every effort to restore an affirmative meaning to 'the universal', not in opposition to 'difference', but by starting from the recognition of 'difference'. For the New Right, the struggle against racism is not won by negating the concept of races, nor by the desire to blend all races into an undifferentiated whole. Rather, the struggle against racism is waged by the refusal of both exclusion and assimilation: neither apartheid nor the melting pot; rather, acceptance of the other as Other through a dialogic perspective of mutual enrichment.

3. Against Immigration; For Cooperation

By reason of its rapid growth and its massive proportions, immigration such as one sees today in Europe constitutes an undeniably negative phenomenon. Essentially, it represents a mode of forced uprooting the cause of which is, first of all, economic — spontaneous or organised movements from poor and overpopulated countries to countries which are rich. But the cause is also symbolic — the attraction of Western civilisation and the concomitant depreciation of indigenous cultures in light of the growing consumer-oriented way of life. The responsibility for current immigration lies primarily, not with the immigrants, but with the industrialised nations which have reduced man to the level of merchandise that can be relocated anywhere. Immigration is not desirable for the immigrants, who are forced to abandon their native country for another where they are received as back-ups for economic needs. Nor is immigration beneficial for the host population receiving the immigrants, who are confronted, against their will, with sometimes brutal modifications in their human and urban environments. It is obvious that the problems of the Third World countries will not be resolved by major population shifts. Thus the New Right favours policies restrictive of immigration, coupled with increased cooperation with Third World countries where organic interdependence and traditional ways of life still survive, in order to overcome imbalances resulting from globalisation.

As regards the immigrant populations which reside today in France, it would be illusory to expect their departure *en masse*. The Jacobin nation-state has always upheld a model of assimilation in which only the individual is absorbed into a citizenship which is purely abstract. The state holds no interest in the collective identities nor in the cultural differences of these individuals. This model becomes less and less credible in view of the following factors: the sheer number of immigrants, the cultural differences which sometimes separate them from the population receiving them, and especially the profound crises which affect all the channels of traditional integration (parties, unions, religions, schools, the army, etc.). The New Right believes that ethnocultural identity should no longer be relegated to the private domain, but should be acknowledged and recognised in the public sphere. The New Right proposes, then, a communitarian model which would spare individuals from being cut off from their cultural roots and which would permit them to keep alive the structures of their collective cultural lives. They should be able to observe necessary general and common laws without abandoning the culture which is their very own. This communitarian politic could, in the long run, lead to a disassociation of citizenship from nationality.

4. Against Sexism; For the Recognition of Gender

The distinction of the sexes is the first and most fundamental of natural differences, for the human race only insures its continuation through this distinction. Being sexual from the very outset, humanity is not one, but rather two. Beyond mere biology, difference inscribes itself in *gender* — masculine and feminine. These determine, in social life, two different ways of perceiving the Other and the world, and they constitute, for individuals, their mode of sexual destiny. The existence of a feminine and masculine nature is evident. However, this does not preclude the fact that individuals of each sex may diverge from these categories due to genetic factors or socio-cultural choices. Nonetheless, in general, a large number of values and attitudes fall into feminine and masculine categories: cooperation and competition, mediation and repression, seduction and domination, empathy and detachment, concrete and abstract, affective and managerial, persuasion and aggression, synthetic intuition and analytic intellection, etc. The modern concept of abstract individuals, detached from their sexual identity, stemming from an 'indifferentialist' ideology which neutralises sexual differences, is just as prejudicial against women as traditional sexism which, for centuries, considered women as incomplete men. This is a twisted form of male domination, which in the past had excluded women from the arena of public life, and admits them today— on the condition that they divest themselves of their femininity.

Some universalist feminists claim that masculine and feminine genders stem from a social construct ('One is not born a woman, one becomes a woman'). In this way, feminism falls into a male-centred trap as it adheres to 'universal' and abstract values which are, in the final analysis, masculine values. The New Right supports a differentialist feminism which, to the contrary, wants sexual difference to play a role in the public domain and upholds specifically feminine rights (the right to virginity, to maternity, to abortion). Against sexism and unisex utopianism, differentialist feminism recognises men as well as women by acknowledging the equal value of their distinct and unique natures.

5. Against the New Class; For Autonomy from the Bottom Up

In the process of globalisation, Western civilisation is promoting the worldwide domination of a ruling class whose only claim to legitimacy resides in its abstract manipulations (logico-symbolic) of the signs and values of the system already in place. Aspiring to uninterrupted growth of capital and to the permanent reign of social engineering, this New Class provides the manpower for the media, large national and multinational firms, and international organisations. This New Class produces and reproduces everywhere the same type of person: cold-blooded specialists, rationality detached from day-to-day realities. It also engenders abstract individualism, utilitarian beliefs, a superficial humanitarianism, indifference to history, an obvious lack of culture, isolation from the real world, the sacrifice of the real to the virtual, an inclination to corruption, nepotism and to buying votes. All of this fits in with the tactic of mergers and the globalisation of worldwide domination. The further that those in power distance themselves from the average citizen, the less they feel the need to justify their decisions. The more a society offers its citizens impersonal tasks to do, the less that society is open to workers of real quality; the less the private domain encroaches upon the public domain, the less are individual achievements recognised and acknowledged by the public; the more one is obliged to 'fulfil a function', the less one is able to 'play a role'. The New Class depersonalises the leadership of Western societies and even lessens their sense of responsibility.

Since the end of the Cold War and the collapse of the Soviet Bloc, the New Class finds itself again confronted with a whole series of conflicts (between capital and labour, equality and freedom, the public and the private) which it had attempted to avoid for over a half a century. Likewise, its ineffectiveness, its wastefulness, and its counter-productivity appear more and more evident. The system tends to close in upon itself, while the public feels indifferent toward or angry at a managerial elite which does not even speak the same language as they do. As regards every major social issue, the gulf widens between the rulers who repeat the usual technocratic discourse and those governed who experience, in their day-to-day lives, the consequences of all this. All the while the media draw attention away from the real world towards one of mere representation. At the highest levels of society, we find technocratic doubletalk, sanctimonious babble, and the comfort of capital yield; at the bottom of the social ladder, the pains of day-to-day life, an incessant search for meaning, and the desire for shared values.

Average citizens have nothing but scorn for the 'elite' and they are indifferent to the traditional political factions and agendas which have today become obsolete. Satisfying the people's (or populist) aspirations would entail giving more autonomy to structures at the lower end of the social ladder, giving them the opportunity to create or recreate specific *nomoi*. In order to create a more 'user-friendly' society, one would have to avoid the anonymity of the masses, the commodification of values, and the reification of social relations. Rather, local communities would have to make decisions by and for themselves in all those matters which concern them directly, and all members would have to participate at every stage of the deliberations and of the democratic decision-making. It is not the Welfare State that ought to decentralise in their favour. Rather, it is the local communities themselves that ought not cede to State power to intervene except in those matters for which they are not able or competent to make decisions.

6. Against Jacobinism; For a Federal Europe

The first Thirty Years War (1618-1648), concluded by the Treaty of Westphalia, marked the establishment of the nation-state as the dominant mode of political organisation. The second Thirty Years' War (1914-45) signalled, to the contrary, the start of the disintegration of the nation-state. Born out of absolute monarchy and revolutionary Jacobinism, the nation-state is now too big to manage little problems and too small to address big ones. In a globalised world, the future belongs to large cultures and civilisations capable of organising themselves into autonomous entities and of acquiring enough power to resist outside interference. Europe must organise itself into a federal structure, while recognising the autonomy of all the component elements and facilitating the cooperation of the constituent regions and of individual nations. European civilisation will remake itself, not by the negation, but by the recognition of historical cultures, thus permitting all inhabitants to rediscover their common origins. The principle of subsidiarity ought to be the keystone at every level. Authority at the lower levels should not be delegated to authorities at the upper levels except in those matters which escape the competence of the lower level.

As opposed to the centralising tradition, which confiscates all powers to establish a single level of control, as opposed to a bureaucratic and technocratic Europe, which relinquishes sovereignty without transferring it to a higher level; as opposed to a Europe which will only be a big market unified by free trade; as opposed to a 'Europe of Nations', a mere assemblage of national egos which cannot prevent future wars; as opposed to a 'European Nation' which is nothing more than a larger version of the Jacobin state; as opposed to all of the above, Europe (Western, Central, and Eastern) must reorganise itself from the bottom up, in close continental association with Russia. The existing states must federalise themselves from within, in order to better federalise with each other. Each level of the association should have its own role and its own dignity, not derived with approval from above, but based on the will and consent of all those who participate. The only decisions that would come from the summit of this structure would be those relating to all the peoples and federal communities: diplomatic matters, military affairs, big economic issues, fundamental legal questions, protection of the environment, etc. European integration is equally necessary in certain areas of research, industry, and new communications technology. A single currency ought to be managed by a central bank under the control of European political authority.

7. Against Depoliticisation; For the Strengthening of Democracy

Democracy did not first appear with the Revolutions of 1776 and 1789. Rather, it has constituted a constant tradition in Europe since the existence of the ancient Greek city and since the time of the ancient German 'freedoms'. Democracy is not synonymous with former 'popular democracies' of the East nor with liberal parliamentary democracy today so prevalent in Western countries. Nor does democracy refer to the political party system. Rather, it denotes a system whereby the people are sovereign. Democracy is not endless discussion and debate, but rather a popular decision in favour of the common good. The people may delegate their sovereignty to managers whom they appoint, but they may not relinquish that sovereignty. Majority rule, exercised through the vote, does not imply that truth necessarily proceeds from majority vote; this is only a technique to assure, as closely as possible, an agreement between the people and their leaders. Democracy is also the system best suited to take care of a society's pluralism: by peaceful resolution of conflicts in ideas and by maintaining a positive relationship between the majority and the minority, and by maintaining freedom of expression for minorities, because the minority could be tomorrow's majority.

In democracy, where the people are the subject of constituent power, the fundamental principle is that of political equality. This principle is quite distinct from that of the legal equality of all people, which can give birth to no form of government (equality of all human beings is an apolitical equality, because it lacks the corollary of any possible inequality). Democratic equality is not an anthropological principle (it tells us nothing about the nature of man); it does not claim that all men are *naturally* equal, but only that all citizens are *politically* equal, because they all belong to the same political body. It is, thus, a substantial equality, based upon belonging or membership. As with all political principles, it implies the possibility of a distinction, in this case between citizens and non-citizens. The essential idea of democracy is neither that of the individual nor of humanity, but rather the idea of a body of citizens politically united into a people. Democracy is the system which situates within the people the source of power's legitimacy and then attempts to achieve, as closely as possible, the common identity of the governors and the governed. The objective, existential difference between the one and other can never be a difference of quality. This common identity is the expression of the identity of the people which, through its representatives, has the opportunity to be politically present through its action and participation in public life. Non-voting and turning one's back on public issues rob democracy of its very meaning.

Today, democracy is threatened by a whole series of offshoots and aberrations: the crisis of representation; the interchangeability of political programs; lack of consultation with the people in cases of major decisions affecting their very lives; corruption and technocracy; the disqualification of political parties, many of which have become machines geared primarily toward their election to office and whose candidates are often chosen only on the basis of their ability to be elected; the dominance of lobbyists upholding their private interests over the common good, etc. Add to all this the fact that the modern model of politics is obsolete: political parties are almost all reformist, while most governments are more or less impotent. 'The seizure of power', or 'political takeover', in the Leninist sense of the term, now leads to nothing. In a world of networks, revolt may be possible, but not revolution.

Renewing the democratic spirit implies not settling for mere representative democracy, but seeking to also put into effect, at every level, a true participatory democracy ('that which affects all the people should be the business of all the people'). In order to achieve this, it will be necessary to stop regarding politics as exclusively a state matter. Each citizen must be involved in the pursuit of the common good. Each common good must be identified and upheld as such. The self-absorbed consumer and the passive spectator-citizen will only become involved by the development of a radically decentralised form of democracy, beginning from the bottom, thereby giving to each citizen a role in the choice and control of his destiny. The procedure of referendum could also be useful. To counteract the overwhelming power of money, the supreme authority in modern society, there must be imposed the widest separation possible between wealth and political power.

8. Against Productivism; For New Forms of Labor

Work (in French *travail*, from the Latin *tripalium*, an instrument of torture) has never occupied a central position in ancient or traditional societies, including those which never practiced slavery. Because it is born out of the constraints of necessity, work does not exercise our freedom, as does the work accomplished wherein an individual may see an expression of himself. It is modernity which, through its productivist goal of totally mobilising all resources, has made of work a value in itself, the principal mode of socialisation, and an illusory form of emancipation and of the autonomy of the individual ('freedom through work'). Functional, rational, and monetised, this is 'heteronomous' work that individuals perform most often by obligation than out of vocation, and this work holds meaning for them only in terms of buying power, which can be counted out and measured. Production serves to stimulate consumption, which is needed as a compensation for time put in working. Work has thus been gradually monetised, forcing individuals to work for others in order to pay those who work for them. The possibility of receiving certain services freely and then reciprocating in some way has totally disappeared in a world where nothing has any value, but everything has a price (i.e., a world in which anything that cannot be quantified in monetary terms is held as negligible or non-existent). In a salaried society, each one gives up his time, more often than not, in trying to earn a living.

Now, due to new technologies, we produce more and more goods and services with constantly fewer workers. In Europe, these gains in productivity result in unemployment and they destabilise some of society's very structures. Such productivity favours capital, which uses unemployment and the relocation of workers to weaken the negotiating power of salaried workers. Thus, today the individual worker is not so much exploited, than rendered more and more useless; exclusion replaces alienation in a world ever globally richer, but where the number of poor people constantly increases (so much for the classic theory of trickle-down economics). Even the possibility of returning to full employment would demand a complete break with productivism and the gradual end of an era where payment by salary is the principal means of integration into social life.

The reduction of the length of the work week is a secular given which makes obsolete the Biblical imperative, 'You will labour by the sweat of your brow'. Negotiated reductions in the length of the work week and the concomitant increase of new workers to share their work ought to be encouraged, as well as the possibility of flexible adjustments (annual leaves, sabbaticals, job training courses, etc.) for every type of 'heteronomous' job: to work less in order to work *better* and in order to have some time for oneself to live and enjoy life. In today's society, the attraction and promise of goods grow ever larger, but increasing also is the number of people whose buying power is stagnating or even diminishing. Thus, it is imperative to gradually disassociate work from income. The possibility must be explored of establishing a fixed minimum stipend or income for every citizen from birth until death and without asking anything in return.

9. Against the Ruthless Pursuit of Current Economic Policies; For an Economy at the Service of the People

Aristotle made a distinction between *economics*, which has as its goal the satisfaction of man's needs, and *chrematistics*, whose ultimate end is production, the earning and appropriation of money. Industrial capitalism has been gradually overtaken by a financial capitalism whose goal is to realise maximum returns in the short run, all to the detriment of the condition of national economies and of the long-term interest of the people. This metamorphosis was brought about by the easy availability of credit, widespread speculation, the issuance of unreliable bonds, widespread indebtedness of individuals, firms, and nations, the dominant role of international investors, mutual funds that seek to make speculative profits, etc. The ubiquity of capital allows the financial markets to control politics. Economies become uncertain and even precarious, while the immense world financial bubble bursts from time to time, sending shockwaves throughout the entire financial network.

Economic thought is, moreover, couched in mathematical formulas which claim to be scientific by excluding any factor that cannot be quantified. Thus, the macroeconomic indices (GDP, GNP, the growth rate, etc.) reveal nothing about the actual condition of a society:

disasters, accidents, or epidemics are here counted as positive, since they stimulate economic activity.

Faced with arrogant wealth, which aims only at growing larger still by capitalising on the inequalities and sufferings that it itself engenders, it is imperative to restore the economy to the service of individuals and their quality of life. The first steps should include: instituting, at an international level, a tax on all financial transactions, to cancelling the debt of Third World countries, and drastically revising the entire system of economic development. Priority should be given to self-sufficiency and to the needs of internal, national and regional markets. There needs to be an end to the international system of the division of labour. Local economies must be freed from the dictates of the World Bank and the IMF. Environmental laws ought to be enacted on an international scale. A way has to be found out of the double impasse of ineffective governmental economies, on the one hand, and hyper-competitive market-oriented economies, on the other, by strengthening a third sector (partnerships, mutual societies, and cooperatives) as well as autonomous organisations of mutual aid based on shared responsibility, voluntary membership, and non-profit organisations.

10. Against Gigantism; For Local Communities

The tendency to over-expansion and concentration produces isolated individuals who are thus more vulnerable and defenceless. Widespread exclusion and social uncertainty are the logical consequences of this system, which has wiped out almost all possibilities of reciprocity and solidarity. Faced with traditional, vertical pyramids of domination that inspire no confidence, faced with bureaucracies that are reaching more and more rapidly their level of incompetence, we enter a world of all sorts of cooperative networks. The former tension between a homogeneous civil society and a monopolistic Welfare State has, little by little, been reduced by the existence today of a whole web of organisations supportive of deliberative and well-functioning communities which are forming at every level of social life: the family, the neighbourhood, the village, the city, the professions and in leisure pursuits. It is only at this local level that one can create a standard of living worthy of human beings, not a fragmented life, and free of the demanding imperatives of speed, mobility and return on investment. This standard of living would be supported by fundamental, shared values, directed at the common good. Solidarity must no longer be seen as the result of an anonymous equality (poorly) guaranteed by the Welfare State, but rather as the result of a reciprocity implemented from the bottom up by organic communities taking charge of such matters as insurance and equitable distribution. Only responsible individuals in responsible communities can establish a social justice which is not synonymous with welfare.

This return to the local community will, by its very nature, return their natural vocation to families to provide education, socialisation, and mutual support. This will, in turn, permit individuals to interiorise social rules and laws which, today, are simply imposed from above and outside. The revitalisation of local communities must also be accompanied by a renaissance of the popular traditions that modernity has largely caused to decline. Even worse, modernity has often tried to 'market' these cultural traditions for the benefit of tourists only ('folkloric' shows). Fostering social interaction and a sense of celebration, such traditions inculcate a sense of life's cycles and provide temporal landmarks. Emphasising rhythmic passing of the ages and of the seasons, great moments in life, and the stages of the passing year, they nourish symbolic imagination and they create a social bond. These traditions are never frozen in time, but are in a constant state of renewal.

11. Against Megalopolis; For Cities on a Human Scale

Urbanism has, for more than fifty years, surrendered to the aesthetic of the ugly: bedroom communities with no horizon; residential areas totally lacking soul; grimy suburbs serving as municipal dumping grounds; endless malls which disfigure the approaches to every city; the proliferation of anonymous 'non-places' given over to visitors who are all in a hurry; downtown areas given over completely to business and stripped of their traditional form of social life (cafés, universities, theatres, cinemas, public parks, etc.); disparate styles of apartment buildings; run-down neighbourhoods, or on the opposite end of the spectrum, neighbourhoods constantly under surveillance by hidden cameras and monitored by citizen patrols; the population shift from rural areas and concomitant urban crowding. They no longer build homes for living in but rather for surviving in an urban environment spoiled by the law of maximum financial return on investment and cold practicality. However, a place is, first and foremost, a link: working, moving about, living are not separate functions, but complex acts encompassing the totality of social life.

The city needs to be rethought as the locus of all our potentialities and the labyrinth of our passions and actions, rather than as the cold, geometric expression of economic order. Architecture and urbanism are practiced in the context of a local history and a particular geography which they should reflect. This would entail the revitalisation of an urbanism rooted in and harmonious with the local community, the revival of regional styles, the development of villages and moderate-sized towns in a network centred upon regional capital cities. It would also imply the opening up of rural areas; the gradual dismantling of bedroom communities and areas that are now strictly used for commercial or business purposes; the elimination of now-ubiquitous advertising; as well as diversification of means of transportation: undoing the current tyranny of the private car, increasing transportation of goods by rail, and revitalising public transportation, taking into consideration ecological imperatives.

12. Against Unbridled Technology; For an Integral Ecology

In a finite world, there are limits to growth. Resources, like growth itself, eventually reach their limit. The rapid generalisation of Western levels of production and consumption throughout the whole world could lead, within several decades, to the depletion of most available resources and to a series of climatic and atmospheric disasters with unforeseen consequences for the human race. The disregard shown for nature, the exponential undermining of biodiversity, the alienation of man by the machine, the depletion of our food supplies, all prove that 'always more' is not synonymous with 'always better'. Various ecological groups have upheld this position, which rejects completely the ideology of unlimited progress. We need to become more aware of our responsibilities as regards the organic and inorganic worlds in which we all move about.

The 'mega-machine' knows only one law — maximum return on investments. This must be countered with the principle of responsibility, which demands that the present generation act in such a way that future generations live in a world which is no less beautiful, no less rich, and no less diverse than the world we know today. We must also affirm the importance of the concrete person over the acquisition of wealth, power, and goods (to be more instead of to have more). Sound ecology calls us to move beyond modern anthropocentrism toward the development of a consciousness of the mutual coexistence of mankind and the cosmos. This 'immanent transcendence' reveals nature as a partner and not as an adversary or object. This does not diminish the unique importance of mankind, but it does deny man his exclusive position that Christianity and classical humanism had assigned to him. Economic *hubris* and Promethean technology must be held in check by a sense of balance and harmony. A worldwide effort must be undertaken to establish binding norms and guidelines for the preservation of biodiversity. Man has obligations to the animal and vegetal world. In like manner, standards must be set worldwide for the reduction of pollution. Firms and corporations which pollute should be taxed in proportion to the damage done. A certain level of de-industrialisation in the field of food-processing might favour local production and consumption as well as diversification of food sources. Approaches sympathetic to the cyclical renewal of natural resources must be sustained in the Third World and given priority in 'developed' societies.

13. For Independence of Thought and a Return to the Discussion of Ideas

Incapable of renewing itself, powerless and disillusioned by the failure of its objectives, modern thought has slowly transformed itself into a form of 'thought police' whose purpose is to excommunicate all those who diverge in any way from the currently dominant ideological dogmas. Former revolutionaries have rallied around the *status quo* while carrying over a taste for purges and anathemas from their former lives. This new form of treachery relies upon the tyranny of public opinion, as fashioned by the media, and takes the form of cleansing hysteria, enervating mawkishness or selective indignation. Rather than trying to understand the approaching new century, they keep rehearsing outdated issues and recycling old arguments, which are nothing more than a means to exclude or to discredit opponents. The reduction of politics to the sound management of increasingly problematic growth excludes the possibility of radically changing society or even the possibility of an open discussion of the ultimate goals of collective action.

Democratic debate thus finds itself reduced to nothing. One no longer discusses, one denounces. One no longer reasons, one accuses. One no longer proves, one imposes. All thoughts, all writings suspected of 'deviation' or even of 'drifting' are represented as consciously or unconsciously sympathetic to ideologies that are held to be highly suspect. Incapable of developing their own ideas or even of refuting the ideas of others, these censors fight not only against stated opinions, but also against supposed intentions. This unprecedented decline of critical thought is still more aggravated in France by Parisian navel-gazing. Thus, we have come to forget the traditional rules of civilised debate. One also begins to forget that freedom of opinion, whose disappearance has largely been met with indifference, allows for no exceptions. Fearing free choice by the people and disdaining their aspirations, one prefers the ignorance of the masses.

The New Right advocates a return to critical thinking and strongly supports total freedom of expression. Faced with censorship, 'disposable' ideas and the futility of passing fads, the New Right insists, now more than ever, on the need for a true renewal of critical thinking. The New Right advocates a return to debating issues, freed from the old divisions and fixed positions which block new approaches to old problems as well as new syntheses. The New Right calls all free minds to join in a common front against the disciples of Trissotin, Tartuffe, and Torquemada.[8]

---

8   Trissotin is a character from the play *The Learned Ladies* by Molière who pretends to be a great scholar in order to become the tutor to a group of women, although his real intention is only to make money from them. Similarly, Tartuffe is a character in a French play of the same name by Molière, written in 1664. In it, Tartuffe is believed to be a man of great religious fervour by others, but he is, in fact, a hypocrite who manipulates others into giving him what he wants. Tomás de Torquemada (1420-1498) was the most infamous Grand Inquisitor of the Spanish Inquisition. -Ed.

Other books published by Arktos:

Beyond Human Rights
by Alain de Benoist

The Problem of Democracy
by Alain de Benoist

Germany's Third Empire
by Arthur Moeller van den Bruck

The Arctic Home in the Vedas
by Bal Gangadhar Tilak

Revolution from Above
by Kerry Bolton

Metaphysics of War
by Julius Evola

The Path of Cinnabar:
An Intellectual Autobiography
by Julius Evola

Archeofuturism
by Guillaume Faye

Why We Fight
by Guillaume Faye

The WASP Question
by Andrew Fraser

The Saga of the Aryan Race
by Porus Homi Havewala

The Owls of Afrasiab
by Lars Holger Holm

De Naturae Natura
by Alexander Jacob

Fighting for the Essence
by Pierre Krebs

Can Life Prevail?
by Pentti Linkola

A Handbook of Traditional Living
by Raido

The Jedi in the Lotus: Star Wars
and the Hindu Tradition
by Steven J. Rosen

It Cannot Be Stormed
by Ernst von Salomon

Tradition & Revolution
by Troy Southgate

Against Democracy and Equality:
The European New Right
by Tomislav Sunic

The Initiate: Journal of Traditional Studies
by David J. Wingfield (ed.)